A special gift to

Kate Brennan

From

Sheilia Plates

Date

December 2013

A Pocket Book of Prayers for Teens

© 2004 Christian Art Gifts, RSA
        Christian Art Gifts Inc., IL, USA

Compiled by Lynette Douglas
Additional prayers by Lynette Douglas
Designed by Christian Art Gifts

Printed in China

ISBN 978-1-86920-147-0

12 13 14 15 16 17 18 19 20 21 – 21 20 19 18 17 16 15 14 13 12

A Pocket Book of Prayers

for Teens

christian
art gifts®

Contents

The Lord's Prayer

Our Father in heaven,
hallowed be your name,
your kingdom come,
your will be done on earth
as it is in heaven.
Give us today our daily bread.
Forgive us our debts,
as we also have
forgiven our debtors.
And lead us not
into temptation,
but deliver us
from the evil one.
Matthew 6:9-13

Confession
and
Purity

A Clean Heart

Father,
Listen to my prayer.
Turn my ways to Your ways;
make me holy,
set my thinking right;
straighten out my desires;
create a pure heart within me;
give me a new and steadfast spirit.

Launcelot Andrewes

Confession

Jesus, You are Lord of my life, and I want to live the way You want me to – but so often I do things that I don't mean to. I make the wrong decisions, or agree with wrong ideas just so I'll fit in. And so often I don't do the things I should do – like being helpful and caring and looking out for those who aren't popular or pretty. Father, forgive me for doing the things I shouldn't do, and for not doing the things I should do.
Amen

Deliver us from Evil

O God, we pray Thee, deliver us
and all men from the power of evil:
from the fears and faithlessness
of our own hearts;
from pride and all forms
of self-deception;
from the misuse of power;
from self-concern and indifference
to the needs of others;
from the blindness which sees no
difference between good and evil;
and from the sloth
that allows evil to pass for good.
When we fail
cast us not from Thy presence,
but let Thy forgiveness restore us
and Thy power make us brave and loyal.

Unknown

An Un**divided** Heart

Teach me Your ways, O Lord my God,
and I will walk in Your truth;
Give me a totally undivided heart;
Cleanse me, Lord, I pray;
Remove from me all that is
standing in the way of Your love.

⟳ Eugene Greco ⟳

For Forgiveness

All that we ought to have thought
and have not thought,
All that we ought to have said
and not said,
All that we ought to have done
and not done,
All that we ought not to have done,
and yet have done,
For these words, and works, pray we,
O God, for forgiveness.

Traditional

Surrounded by Sin

Lord, everywhere I turn there are things that look like fun but that I know are wrong.

I am surrounded by sin on every side. "Just say no!" they say – but it isn't always that easy.

Sometimes the kids who are doing bad things look like they're having so much fun.

And I try not to long to join them. Lord, I know You have made so many great things for us to enjoy.

And there are so many ways to have a good time that aren't wrong.

Help me not to feel deprived and out of it – and give me the strength to follow You with all my heart, always and forever.

Amen

The Lie I Told

Father, I told a lie this morning. It seemed the easiest way to deal with the situation I was in, but all day long I have felt uneasy about it. Is that my conscience pricking me?

I wonder if I will be caught out, and will that be worse than if I had told the truth from the start? You honor the truth – for You are the Truth.

Help me to honor the truth too, to realize that it is the basis of integrity, and that if I become known as someone who tells lies then others won't trust or respect me.

The lie I told didn't seem a big deal at first, but then I realize how much I rely on untruths and evasions to try to make things easier for myself.

Lord, forgive me for each lie I have ever told, for leaving out certain facts when I tell a story or give an explanation that put a different slant on the truth, for the times when I've said I couldn't do something, when I really could.

Help me to walk in Your truth always, and take responsibility for my every action.

Amen

Knowing
God

The Lord Knows

O LORD, you have searched me and you know me. You know when I sit and when I rise; you perceive my thoughts from afar. You discern my going out and my lying down; you are familiar with all my ways. Before a word is on my tongue you know it completely, O LORD. You hem me in – behind and before; you have laid your hand upon me.

Such knowledge is too wonderful for me, too lofty for me to attain. How precious to me are your thoughts, O God! How vast is the sum of them! Were I to count them, they would outnumber the grains of sand. When I awake, I am still with you.

Psalm 139:1-6, 17-18

To Love Him Above All Things

O God, who hast prepared
for them that love Thee
such good things
as pass man's understanding;
Pour into our hearts
such love toward Thee,
that we, loving Thee
above all things,
may obtain Thy promises,
which exceed all that we can desire;
through Jesus Christ our Lord.
Amen

⇒ The Book of Common Prayer ⇐

More Than Conquerors

Who shall separate us from the love
of Christ? Shall trouble or hardship or
persecution or famine or nakedness
or danger or sword? As it is written:
"For your sake we face death all day
long; we are considered as sheep to be
slaughtered." No, in all these things we
are more than conquerors through him
who loved us.

For I am convinced that neither death
nor life, neither angels nor demons,
neither the present nor the future, nor
any powers, neither height nor depth, nor
anything else in all creation, will be able
to separate us from the love of God that is
in Christ Jesus our Lord.

Romans 8:35-39

I Long to Enjoy You

O Lord,
I called You
and longed to enjoy You,
and I am prepared
to give up everything for You.
Let my mouth,
my soul, and all creation
praise and bless You!
Amen

Thomas à Kempis

God's Great Love

I call on you, O God, for you
     will answer me;
  give ear to me and
     hear my prayer.
Show the wonder of
     your great love,
  you who save by
     your right hand
  those who take refuge in you
     from their foes.
Keep me as the apple of
     your eye;
  hide me in the
     shadow of your wings
from the wicked who assail me,
  from my mortal enemies who
     surround me.

Psalm 17:6-9

Psalm 91

He who dwells in the shelter of the Most High will rest in the shadow of the Almighty. I will say of the LORD, "He is my refuge and my fortress, my God, in whom I trust."

If you make the Most High your dwelling – even the Lord, who is my refuge – then no harm will befall you, no disaster will come near your tent. For he will command his angels concerning you to guard you in all your ways; they will lift you up in their hands, so that you will not strike your foot against a stone. You will tread upon the lion and the cobra; you will trample the great lion and the serpent.

Psalm 91:1-2, 9-13

When God Seems Far Away

Lord, I know Your Word says that You are with us always – but sometimes it seems as if You are far, far away from my life. I can't see You or feel You or hear You. I want to believe, but believing just seems too hard.

O God, I do believe, help my unbelief. I want to know You more, to love You more, but my heart feels dry and empty. So I will pray, and wait for You to refresh me with Your Living Water and cause a new season of growth and gladness in my heart.

Amen

"If you remain in me
and my words remain in you,
ask whatever you wish,
and it will be given you."

John 15:7

Lord, Open Unto Me

Open unto me:

† light for my darkness.
† courage for my fear.
† hope for my despair.
† peace for my turmoil.
† joy for my sorrow.
† strength for my weakness.
† wisdom for my confusion.
† forgiveness for my sins.
† tenderness for my toughness.
† love for my hates.
† Thy Self for my self.

Lord, Lord, open unto me!
Amen

Howard Thurman

When Reading the Bible

O Lord,
wash over me
with the refreshing waters
of Your Word.
Wash away the dirt
and dust of today
and fill me
with life and freshness.
Sow the seeds
of Your Word
deep in my heart
and let them grow
into the precious fruit
of Your Spirit.
Amen

God At the Center

O God,
Sometimes I get so caught up
in the things of my life
that I forget about You,
I push You
to the perimeter of my life
instead of making You the center.
Forgive me
for thinking about You
only when I'm stuck
and need some help.
Help me to readjust my priorities
and put You at the center.
Always.
Amen

Fill Me

Breathe on me, Breath of God,
Fill me with life anew,
That I may love what Thou dost love,
And do what Thou wouldst do.

⟞ Edwin Hatch ⟝

The Lord's Great Love

Lord,
Today I thought again
about what You did
for us on the cross.
When I think of Your great love,
and my unworthiness,
I am overwhelmed.
And there is nothing
I can say except
Thank You, Thank You, Thank You.

Do not be anxious about anything,
but in everything,
by prayer and petition,
with thanksgiving,
present your requests to God.
And the peace of God,
which transcends all understanding,
will guard your hearts
and your minds in Christ Jesus.

⁓ Philippians 4:6-7 ⁓

Spiritual
Growth

Strength of Love

I pray that out of his glorious riches he
may strengthen you with power through
his Spirit in your inner being, so that
Christ may dwell in your hearts.

And I pray that you, being rooted and
established in love, may have power,
together with all the saints, to grasp how
wide and long and high and deep is the
love of Christ, and to know this love
that surpasses knowledge – that you may
be filled to the measure of all the fullness
of God.

Ephesians 3:16-19

The Way Everlasting

Search me,
O God search me
and know my heart,
try me and prove me
in the hidden part;
cleanse me
and make me
holy as Thou art,
and lead me
in the way everlasting.

A. B. Simpson

Spiritual Growth

Lead us from death to life,
from falsehood to truth.
Lead us from despair to hope,
from fear to trust.
Lead us from hate to love,
from war to peace.
Let peace fill our heart, our world,
our universe.

∽ Anglican Prayer ∽

Guidance

Show me your ways, O Lord,
   teach me your paths;
guide me in your truth
     and teach me,
   for you are God my Savior,
   and my hope is in you
     all day long.
Remember, O Lord, your great
     mercy and love,
   for they are from of old.
Remember not the sins
    of my youth
   and my rebellious ways;
according to your love
     remember me,
   for you are good, O Lord.

∽ Psalm 25:4-7 ∽

Through the Storm

Take my hand,
precious Lord,
lead me on,
let me stand.
I am tired, I am weak, I am worn.
Through the storm,
through the night,
lead me on to the light.
Take my hand,
precious Lord,
lead me home.

Thomas Dorsey

Psalm 23

The LORD is my shepherd, I shall not be in want. He makes me lie down in green pastures, he leads me beside quiet waters, he restores my soul. He guides me in paths of righteousness for his name's sake.

Even though I walk through the valley of the shadow of death, I will fear no evil, for you are with me; your rod and your staff, they comfort me. You prepare a table before me in the presence of my enemies.

You anoint my head with oil; my cup overflows. Surely goodness and love will follow me all the days of my life, and I will dwell in the house of the LORD forever.

⸜ Psalm 23 ⸝

The LORD is near
to all who call on him,
to all who call
on him in truth.
He fulfills the desires
of those who fear him;
he hears their cry
and saves them.

Psalm 145:18-19

Solomon's Prayer for Wisdom

You have shown great kindness to your servant, my father David, because he was faithful to you and righteous and upright in heart. You have continued this great kindness to him and have given him a son to sit on his throne this very day. Now, O LORD my God, you have made your servant king in place of my father David.

But I am only a little child and do not know how to carry out my duties. Your servant is here among the people you have chosen, a great people, too numerous to count or number. So give your servant a discerning heart to govern your people and to distinguish between right and wrong. For who is able to govern this great people of yours?

1 Kings 3:6-9

Wisdom and Understanding

We have not stopped praying for you and asking God to fill you with the knowledge of his will through all spiritual wisdom and understanding.

And we pray this in order that you may live a life worthy of the Lord and may please him in every way:

bearing fruit in every good work,

growing in the knowledge of God,

being strengthened with all power according to his glorious might

so that you may have great endurance and patience,

and joyfully giving thanks to the Father, who has qualified you to share in the inheritance of the saints in the kingdom of light.

Colossians 1:9-12

Open the Eyes of our Heart

I keep asking that the God of our Lord Jesus Christ, the glorious Father, may give you the Spirit of wisdom and revelation, so that you may know him better.

I pray also that the eyes of your heart may be enlightened in order that you may know the hope to which he has called you, the riches of his glorious inheritance in the saints, and his incomparably great power for us who believe.

Ephesians 1:17-19

The Right Path

Dear God,
Help me to take the right path in life and
help me to know right from wrong.
Show me a way
to get through life and its problems
no matter how hard they are.
Help me to build a life
I can be proud of and
show me the way to make a happy life.
I put my trust in You
as You are a God who loves
us no matter who we are.

Craig Adams

Strength in the Lord

In me there is darkness,
but with You there is light;
I am lonely, but You do not leave me;
I am feeble in heart,
but with You there is help;
I am restless, but with You there is peace.
In me there is bitterness,
but with You there is patience;
I do not understand Your ways,
but You know the way for me.
Lord Jesus Christ,
You were poor and in distress,
a captive and forsaken as I am.
You know all man's troubles; You abide
with me when all men fail me;
You remember and seek me;
it is Your will that I should know
You and turn to You.
Lord, I hear Your call and follow.
Help me.

Dietrich Bonhoeffer

God Be With Me

God be in my head,
and in my understanding;
God be in my eyes,
and in my looking;
God be in my mouth
and in my speaking;
God be in my heart,
and in my thinking;
God be at my end,
and at my departing.

Traditional

Growing Up

Lord, so often this path from childhood to adulthood is rocky and hard. Some days I feel like a kid – unsure of who I am or what I want from life. Other days I feel ready to take on the world and do great things.

Sometimes I think I know the answers to life and other times I'm not even sure that I know the questions. Some days I want to be independent and do things on my own, and then suddenly I get scared of leaving childhood behind and having to make my own decisions. I need a guide through the uncertainties ahead of me. I need a chart through strange seas before me. I need a light to show me the way. Lord, You are the Way and the Truth and the Life.

Be with me as I grow toward adulthood, I pray.

Amen

Life and Purpose

I have life before me still
and Thy purpose to fulfill;
yea a debt to pay Thee yet:
Help me, Lord, and so I will.

Gerard Manly Hopkins

Making Decisions

God, who promises to lead and guide us into all truth, to show us the way through life, so that we can enter life-everlasting, give me wisdom and understanding so that I can make the right decisions at the right time.

It is so easy to go with the flow – to be one of the crowd and let them make my choices for me.

But often those choices go against Your goodness or even my own desires.

Teach me to walk in Your ways and to be true to myself.

Amen

On **Wings of** Faith

Lord of all the big and the small, as I start spreading my wings and flying free, help me not to be afraid of the unknown world I will encounter "out there."

A world of new experiences, of so much possibility, and where my potential can develop and grow.

A world of new opportunities and new experiences. Help me to soar on wings of faith, and ride high on the currents of Your grace.

Help me not to be afraid of trying my wings in new directions, under Your guidance. In Jesus' name.

Amen

A New Thing

Dear God, the world is full of new things –
new days, new friends, new ideas
to think about, new opportunities to
explore.

The future lies before me like a great
uncharted continent. You have promised
to be my Good Shepherd and to guide me
by still waters and into green fields.

Lord, guide me along the paths of
righteousness, for Your name's sake.

And let goodness and love follow me
all the days of my life.

Amen

Consecration
and
Service

Serving God

Teach us, Lord,
to serve You as You deserve,
to give and not to count the cost,
to fight and not to heed the wounds,
to toil and not to seek for rest,
to labor and not to ask for any reward
save that of knowing
that we do Your will.

Ignatius of Loyola

A Life to Proclaim Him

O gracious and holy Father,
give us wisdom to perceive Thee,
intelligence to understand Thee,
diligence to seek Thee,
patience to wait for Thee,
eyes to behold Thee,
a heart to meditate upon Thee,
and a life to proclaim Thee;
through the power of the Spirit
of Jesus Christ our Lord.

～ St. Benedict ～

A Prayer for Doing Good

Dear Lord,
I shall pass through this world but once;
any good, therefore, that I can do
or any kindness that I can show to any
fellow creature
let me do it now;
let me not defer or neglect it,
for I shall not pass this way again.

∽ Stephen Grellet ∽

Commitment to Service

Lord Jesus,
take me this day and use me.
Take my lips
and speak through them.
Take my mind
and think through it.
Take my will
and act through it,
and fill my heart
with love for You.

Traditional

Use Me, Lord

Use me, my Savior, for whatever purpose
and in whatever way You may require.
Here is my poor heart, an empty vessel:
fill it with Your grace. Here is my sinful
and troubled soul; quicken it and freshen
it with Your love.

Take my heart for Your abode; my
mouth to spread abroad the glory of Your
name; my love and all my powers for the
advancement of Your believing people,
and never allow the steadfastness and
confidence of my faith to abate.

⌒ Dwight L. Moody ⌒

Consecration of Gifts to the Lord

You take the pen
and the lines dance.
You take the flute
and the notes shimmer.
You take the brush
and the colors sing.
So all things have
meaning and beauty
in that space beyond time
where You are.
How, then, can I
hold back anything from You?

Dag Hammarskjöld

Surrender

Lord, we do not know
what this life
has in store for us,
but be it good or bad,
we are willing
to be used by You.
Use us
until that moment comes
when we go from
service good to service best –
when You begin to use us in glory!

Corrie ten Boom

Instruments of Peace

Lord, make me an instrument of Thy peace.

Where there is hatred, let me sow love;
where there is injury, pardon;
where there is doubt, faith;
where there is despair, hope;
where there is darkness, light;
and where there is sadness, joy.

O Divine Master, grant that I may not so much seek to be consoled as to console;

to be understood as to understand;
For it is in giving that we receive;
it is in pardoning that we are pardoned;
and it is in dying that we are born to eternal life.

Francis of Assisi

Make us Worthy, Lord

Make us worthy, Lord,
to serve others throughout the world
who live and die in poverty or hunger;
Give them through our hands, this day
their daily bread,
and by our understanding love,
give peace and joy.
Amen

⟶ Mother Teresa ⟵

Consecration

Take my life and let it be
consecrated, Lord, to Thee.
Take my moments and my days;
Let them flow in ceaseless praise.
Take my will, and make it Thine,
it shall be no longer mine.
Take my heart – it is Thine own;
It shall be Thy royal throne.

⮞ Frances Ridley Havergal ⮜

Joy in Giving

Make us ever eager, Lord,
to share the good things that we have.
Grant us such a measure
of Thy Spirit that we may find
more joy in giving than in getting.
Make us ready
to give cheerfully without grudging,
secretly without praise,
and in sincerity
without looking for gratitude,
for Jesus Christ's sake.
Amen

John Hunter

To be a Witness

Precious Lord,
You have asked us
to share Your love with others,
to introduce those
who do not know You
to Your goodness and mercy.
There are so many people
I meet each day
who never think about You – except
when they use Your name in vain.
You called us
to talk about You,
to be Your witnesses.
Fill me with boldness
and wisdom to know
what to say so that others
will find out how much
You love them, too.
Amen

Intercession
and
Petition

A Call for Mercy

Hear, O LORD, and answer me, for I am poor and needy. Guard my life, for I am devoted to you. You are my God; save your servant who trusts in you.

Have mercy on me, O LORD, for I call to you all day long. Bring joy to your servant, for to you, O LORD, I lift up my soul.

You are forgiving and good, O LORD, abounding in love to all who call to you. Hear my prayer, O LORD; listen to my cry for mercy. In the day of my trouble I will call to you, for you will answer me.

Teach me your way, O Lord, and I will walk in your truth; give me an undivided heart, that I may fear your name.

I will praise you, O Lord my God, with all my heart; I will glorify your name forever. For great is your love toward me; you have delivered me from the depths of the grave.

Psalm 86:1-7, 11-13

Refuge in the Lord

In you, O LORD, I have taken refuge; let me never be put to shame. Rescue me and deliver me in your righteousness; turn your ear to me and save me. Be my rock of refuge, to which I can always go; give the command to save me, for you are my rock and my fortress. Deliver me, O my God, from the hand of the wicked, from the grasp of evil and cruel men.

For you have been my hope, O Sovereign Lord, my confidence since my youth. From birth I have relied on you; you brought me forth from my mother's womb. I will ever praise you.

My mouth is filled with your praise, declaring your splendor all day long.

Psalm 71:1-6, 8

Peace to Our World

Creator of the world,
help us love one another,
help us care for each other
as sister or brother,
that friendship may grow
from nation to nation.
Bring peace to our world
O Lord of creation.

Unknown

For a Better World

I call down Thy blessing today
upon all who are striving toward
the making of a better world.
I pray, O God, especially
for all who are valiant for truth,
for all who are working
for purer and juster laws,
for all who are working
for peace between nations,

for all who are engaged
in healing disease,
for all who are engaged
in the relief of poverty,
for all who are engaged
in the rescue of the fallen,
for all who preach the gospel,
for all who bear witness to Christ
in foreign lands,
for all who suffer
for righteousness' sake.
Cast down, O Lord,
all the forces of cruelty and wrong.
Defeat all selfish
and worldly-minded schemes,
and prosper all
that is conceived among us
in the Spirit of Christ
and carried out to the honor
of His blessed name.
Amen

John Baillie

"Before they call
I will answer;
while they are still speaking
I will hear."

Isaiah 65:24

A Prayer for My Teachers

God of all wisdom and understanding, I know that my teachers are wise and they know their stuff, but so often I find it hard to understand the things they're teaching. And then I get frustrated, and often I think the homework they give us is a waste of time.

But Lord, then I see how they help us with other things too, with sports and clubs, and I see how they give their time when they don't need to, and I appreciate them. Lord, hear my prayer today, and give them more patience, and me more ability to concentrate.

And help me to remember that the work they give us has a purpose beyond today, beyond this week, beyond even this year.

Amen

No Answer

God, remember that thing
I prayed about a while ago?
I hoped for an answer,
but so far
there hasn't been one.
Not yet.
Lord,
I know sometimes
Your silences
speak louder than answers.
Help me to hear
what You are saying to me
as I wait, and hope, and believe.
Amen

Disappointment

God, I prayed and prayed ... and now I
know that what I prayed for isn't going to
happen the way I wanted it to. I feel so let
down ... so disappointed ... so flat inside.

I know the Bible says that everything
works out for the best if only we believe
You – but it doesn't feel that way
right now. I can't see the best in this
disappointment.

Help me, Lord, to accept the things
that have happened and to make the
most of how they've turned out. Help me
not to stay discouraged.

Amen

Family
and
Friends

Mom and Me

O God, please forgive me.

I've done it again – gone and got into an argument with Mom. I don't mean to, but somehow I end up saying all kinds of things I don't really mean.

I do love her, and I don't mean to hurt her with the things I say.

Help me to forgive her, and help her to forgive me, too.

Lord, fill our hearts with words that will help and not hurt, with words that will build up and not tear down.

And give me the courage and strength to apologize.

Amen

Being "Cool"

Sometimes I think it would be great to be one of the cool kids – one of the popular kids always getting asked to parties and who seem to have it all together.

Sometimes I feel like such a dunce – like nothing I do is important or worthwhile. I don't seem to shine at anything – just average – that's me – average looks, average grades, average everything.

But then, Lord, I hear the whisper of Your Spirit in my heart telling me that I am precious in Your sight and You made me special.

Help me to appreciate the unique things about me that You created, and help me to be happy to be me.

Amen

When Friends Hurt

Dear Lord Jesus, I thought that we would be friends forever – that we would look out for each other and help each other – but now my friend has found a new best friend, and I feel betrayed and left out.

I guess I feel a little of the pain and rejection You felt when Your friends left You and betrayed You, and I pray that You would help me remember that You did that for me so that I never have to be completely alone – You are always with me.

Amen

Dating

Lord, just as You care about the other parts of my life, You care about who I date and who dates me! It's great to go out and to think about falling in love.

It's great to feel special, and loved. Let me not get so caught up in romance that I forget about genuine love.

Be with us as we spend time together – whatever we do, whether we go to movies or out for dinner, or even if we dance.

Help me to keep my ways pure, to remember that You are with me always, that respect is important in good relationships.

Amen

When Angry and Hurt

Lord, I feel so angry and torn up inside.
They say that words can't harm you – but
they do. More deeply and more hurtful
than a slap in the face.

I feel so broken and bleeding inside.
Everything in me wanted to lash out, but
I didn't. I smiled and pretended to join in
the joke, but inside I felt like crying.

You ask us to forgive, but my heart
feels so battered that I can't stop feeling
angry. What should I do? Just let it
pass? Or march in there and insist on an
apology? Help me to see my friend (so-
called) the way You do – as someone who
said something unkind without thinking.
Then, maybe, I will be able to forgive,
and forget.

Amen

Friends

Jesus – the greatest friend in all the world,
You know how great it is to have friends –
just to hang out together and to laugh
and to talk about nothing.
Thanks for friendship and friends.
Thanks for people who let me be just me.
And who like me as I am.
Thanks for being my special Friend.
Amen

Peer Pressure

O God, all around us are things that lead us into temptation – and people who mock when we want to stay pure and healthy for Your sake – and for our own sakes, too.

Help me not to give into the temptations of beer and cigarettes, teen sex, fast cars. You are the God of abundant life. In You is all we need.

Help me not to listen to the voices of movies and magazines and TV – but to what You say.

And Lord, I particularly pray for some of my friends ... You know ... the ones who are really struggling with these things.

Amen

Family

Father God, You created families.
You put us together as a family –
Dad and Mom, brothers and sisters,
aunts and uncles, grandpas and grannies,
cousins of all sorts.
Bless our family.
Help us to be together
in unity in all things.
Help us to stick together in love.
Teach us to love each other
with Your love
so that others can see
that when You use the word *family*,
it means *love*.
Amen

Everyday Things

Help for Daily Living

Dear God, You constantly pour out Your blessings on us: help us to be a blessing to others.

You gave us our hands: help us to use them to work for You.

You gave us our feet: help us to use them to walk in Your ways.

You gave us our voices: help us to use them to speak gentleness and truth.

You gave us our minds: help us to think only pleasant, kind thoughts.

You have made our lives pleasant every day with love: help us to make others' lives happier every day with our love.

Help us to please You, Lord. Help us to learn; some little deed to thank You with, instead of words; some little prayer to do instead of say; some little thing to give You because You never tire of giving us so much.

Amen

Unknown

At Day's End

O Lord my God, thank You for bringing this day to a close; thank You for giving me rest in body and soul.

Your hand has been over me and has guarded and preserved me.

Forgive my lack of faith and any wrong that I have done today, and help me to forgive all who have wronged me.

Let me sleep in peace under Your protection, and keep me from the temptations of darkness.

Into Your hands I commend my loved ones and all who dwell in this house.

I commend to You my body and soul.

O God, Your holy name be praised.

Amen

Dietrich Bonhoeffer

Make Our Lives Count

Father, bless to our hearts
this word from Your Word.
Help us to make our lives
count for You.
Help us to serve You
with the strength of youth
... and the strength of age.
And take us at last into Your presence,
Through Jesus Christ our Lord.

Louis Benes

A Clear Vision

Dear Lord,
give us a clear vision
that we may know
where to stand
and what to stand for,
because unless
we stand for something,
we shall fall for anything.

Peter Marshall

In the Morning

Good morning, Lord. It's the start of a brand new day. I rejoice because this is the day You have made and I will be glad in it.

Everything I have to do today I will be able to do well because I can do all things through the strength You give me. You promised to help those who call on Your name, and so I know that all things will go well today.

I want to seek Your Kingdom first in everything today, knowing that as I do so all things will work together for my good, because I love You!

Amen

Lord, Be with Us

Lord, be with us this day.
Within us to purify us;
Above us to draw us up;
Beneath us to sustain us;
Before us to lead us;
Behind us to restrain us;
Around us to protect us.

St. Patrick

Weekends

Lord, I love the weekends – I love Saturday mornings when I can get up late and hang out with my friends.

I love Saturday night movies and popcorn.

I love Sunday school and church on Sunday.

I love having time-out to think and be and just do nothing.

But Lord, the weekend is also filled with all kinds of activities that could sometimes make me forget to set aside time to be with You.

Help me to make good choices this weekend, to have fun in ways that You would approve of, to enjoy myself and yet not do anything that would hurt me or others.

Help me not to forget You while I'm having fun.

Amen

The New School Year

Lord, I feel so excited this morning – I love being at the start of something new – new grade, new teachers, new things to learn, new friends, new books, new clothes.

Going into a new grade makes me feel much more grown up than I did at the end of last semester. I have such good intentions for this year – to work hard and get good grades – to get involved in clubs and activities – to make a good impression on others – to make their lives better because of the things I do.

Lord, I commit this year to You and ask that You will lead me in all things so that I will honor and glorify You in everything I do.

Amen

For the Animals

Dear Father, hear and bless
the beasts and singing birds
and guard with tenderness,
small things that have no words.

~Unknown~

For Animals

Hear our humble prayer, O God,
for our friends the animals.
We entreat for them
all Thy mercy and pity,
and for those who deal with them
we ask a heart of compassion,
gentle hands and kindly words.
Make us ourselves
to be true friends to animals
and so to share
the blessing of the merciful.
For the sake of Thy Son,
the tender-hearted,
Jesus Christ our Lord.

Russian Prayer

A Healthy Body

Dear God, I was amazed this evening when I watched a TV program about the human body. You are an awesome Creator! Who but You could even have imagined a system so intricate, so detailed, so perfectly balanced? Help me to look after my body, to treat it right, not to stuff it full of junk food and other toxins.

Give me the strength to exercise it in ways that will make it the best temple for Your Holy Spirit it can be.

Help me to appreciate the beauty of Your creation without obsessing about being too thin or focusing too much on outward appearances, because, after all, it really is what's inside that counts in the long run, right?

Amen

A Bad Attitude

Lord, do You know how hard it is sometimes to keep a positive attitude?

To be cheerful and kind, when I just want to sulk?

How hard it is to be respectful and obedient when I get tired and want to do my own thing?

God, keep me from getting grouchy and moody.

Forgive me for my bad attitude and help me to grow in the fruit of Your Spirit, to become more and more like You.

Amen

Rejoice in the Lord always.
I will say it again: Rejoice!
Philippians 4:4

Before Taking a Test

Lord, I have a test today. I have worked for it, but maybe not as hard as I should have.

I try and try and try to remember everything I need to know, but sometimes the facts just don't stay in place.

Help me to understand the questions my teacher asks, and help me to remember the things I learned and help me to write answers that are clear and good.

Amen

Let us then approach
the throne of grace with confidence,
so that we may receive
mercy and find grace
to help us in our time of need.

⌒ Hebrews 4:16 ⌒

When I Fail

Beloved Lord, everlasting Father, I messed up today. Will You forgive me for each failure? Do You understand my weaknesses and my sinfulness?

Forgive me, Lord, as You forgive me each time I fail, without ever turning Your back on me. No matter how many times I fail, You are with me.

You never leave me, and You never stop believing that I can and will do better. With Your help, I will go on. With Your help, I can try again.

Amen

Sport

Lord, thanks for making it possible for us to take part in sports. It's great to run and jump and feel muscles stretch and grow strong.

Help me to do the best I can – to work as hard for practices as I do for the actual games.

And, Lord, help me especially to not mind so much whether we win or lose, but to focus on enjoying the game.

May my coach and teammates see You in me through the way I play each game.

Amen

In Success

Father God, I humbly bow before You – the great and awesome God, Creator of all things. And I praise You today for the success that has come my way – I prayed, and planned, and prepared – and it's all worked out! Hallelujah!

Help me, as I rejoice in this success, not to forget that all gifts, abilities, and talents come from You – and You have given me all these so that I can use them to bring glory and honor to You.

Thank You for surrounding me with people – teachers, parents, coaches, friends – who encouraged me and helped me to do the very best. It feels so good to have worked hard and achieved much. Thank You, Lord.

Amen

My Job

Lord, thank You for the privilege of being able to work and to earn my own money.

Help me to do my best at all times – no matter how dreary or hard the work gets.

Help me to be responsible, help me to see what needs to be done and do it.

Help me to be respectful to my boss. And bless me as I work. Grant me Your favor and blessing.

Help me to honor You so that even if I say little, people can see that I serve You.

Amen

Youth Meeting

Lord, I pray that as we come together this evening that friendships will be deepened – both with each other and with You.

Bless our leaders as they help us to grow in the knowledge of You and in holiness.

Bless the projects that we're focusing on. And help us to welcome new kids as You would welcome them.

Amen

Responsibility

Lord, sometimes I do stupid things that risk blowing the independence and trust that I have been given – I risk throwing away the freedom and the responsibility that my parents and others have given me. Why do I abuse these privileges?

Lord, I'm praying that You would help me to keep my head straight – that You would help me to do the right thing even when I think no one is watching. I do want to be responsible and trustworthy.

Help me to think straight before I do anything stupid.

Forgive me for being so dumb – even when I know better.

Amen.

Praise
and
Thanksgiving

Praise the Lord

Praise the LORD, O my soul;
   all my inmost being, praise
      his holy name.
Praise the LORD, O my soul,
   and forget not all
      his benefits –
who forgives all your sins
   and heals all your diseases,
who redeems your life
      from the pit
   and crowns you with love
      and compassion,
who satisfies your desires
      with good things
   so that your youth is renewed
      like the eagle's.

∽ Psalm 103:1-5 ∽

The Gifts of God's Goodness

For this new morning and its light,
For rest and shelter of the night,
For health and food, for love and friends,
For every gift Your goodness sends,
We thank You, gracious Lord.

⧫ Unknown ⧫

Thank You

Thank You, Lord, thank You.
Thank You for the tranquil night.
Thank You for the stars.
Thank You for the silence.
Thank You for the time
You have given me.
Thank You for life.
Thank You for grace.
Thank You for being there, Lord.
Thank You for listening to me,
for taking me seriously,
for gathering my gifts in Your
hands to offer them to Your Father.
Thank You, Lord.
Thank You.

Michel Quoist

Glory to the Lord

Glory to our ascended Lord that He is with us always.

Glory to the Word of God, going forth, with His armies conquering and to conquer.

Glory to Him who has led captivity captive and given gifts for the perfecting of His saints.

Glory to Him who has gone before to prepare a place in His Father's home for us.

Glory to the Author and the Finisher of our faith; that God in all things may be glorified through Jesus Christ, to whom be all worship and praise, dominion and glory; now and forever and ever.

Amen

∽ Sursum Corda ∽

God is Faithful

Let us with gladsome mind
praise the Lord for He is kind;
For His mercies shall endure,
ever faithful, ever sure.

 ∽ *John Milton* ∽

A Song of Praise

My heart rejoices in the LORD;
in the LORD my horn is lifted high.
My mouth boasts over my enemies,
for I delight in your deliverance.
There is no one holy like the LORD;
there is no one besides you;
there is no Rock like our God.
He raises the poor from the dust
and lifts the needy from the ash heap;
he seats them with princes
and has them inherit a throne of honor.
For the foundations of the earth
are the LORD's;
upon them he has set the world.
He will guard the feet of his saints.

∽ *1 Samuel 2:1-2, 8-9* ∽

Exalt the Lord

Blessed be your glorious name,
and may it be exalted
above all blessing and praise.
You alone are the LORD.
You made the heavens,
even the highest heavens,
and all their starry host,
the earth and all that is on it,
the seas and all that is in them.
You give life to everything,
and the multitudes
of heaven worship you.

Nehemiah 9:5-6

Thank You

Lord, this morning when I woke up I felt
a flood of thankfulness flow through me.
This is such a great morning! The sun is
shining, the birds are singing, and I can
smell the pancakes and bacon Mom is
making for breakfast. I want to sing out a
song of thanks to You this morning –

Thanks for sunshine and birds.

Great food that tastes as good
as it smells.

Friends who make good times
extra fun.

Blue skies and fresh green grass.

Family that loves and loves and loves.

Hugs and laughter, stillness and peace,

and specially for loving me enough to
make me Your child.

Amen

A Great Day

What an amazing,
stupendous, glorious,
wonderful day this has been!
Father of all that is good
and great and glorious,
thank You
for Your innumerable blessings.
Amen and amen.

For Simple Things

Lord, so often I forget to appreciate the really simple things – things like fresh water and sunshine and friendly smiles and birds singing.

It's so easy to get caught up in the things like more clothes, more CDs, more shoes – to put too much value on things and possessions instead of the really important things in life – like friendship and health and family.

So today I want to thank You for the simple things. For the good things. For the great things You supply.

Amen

When Camping Out

Great and mighty God, Creator of all things both big and small, here we are surrounded by all the magnificence and magnitude and majesty of the world You created: the great open skies and bright fiery stars, the serene green trees and the brightly colored flowers, the river that flows both fast and slow.

It is such a blessing to be out here. Lord, our Lord, how majestic are the works of Your hands.

Amen

The Glory of the Lord

How many are your works, O Lord! In wisdom you made them all; the earth is full of your creatures.

These all look to you to give them their food at the proper time.

When you give it to them, they gather it up; when you open your hand, they are satisfied with good things.

May the glory of the Lord endure forever; may the Lord rejoice in his works – I will sing to the Lord all my life; I will sing praise to my God as long as I live.

Psalm 104:24, 27-28, 31, 33